Build Your Own
Wire Pendants

Here is the pendant that inspired this book. I fell in love with this small but gorgeous hot-pink cobaltocalcite drusy cabochon and built a frame, made a bail, and added embellishment to show it off.

Build Your Own
Wire Pendants

Kimberly Sciaraffa Berlin

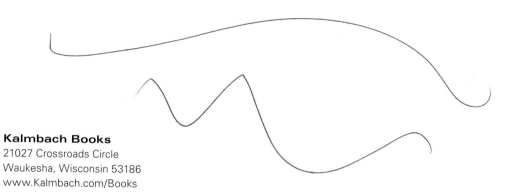

Kalmbach Books
21027 Crossroads Circle
Waukesha, Wisconsin 53186
www.Kalmbach.com/Books

Lead photography © 2012 Kalmbach Books. Lettered step-by-step and design options photos by Jeff Ramirez.

The jewelry designs in *Build Your Own Wire Pendants* are the copyrighted property of the author, and they may not be taught without permission. You may produce work for sale based on the techniques presented if you give credit to the author/designer and the book.

Published in 2012

17 16 15 14 13   3 4 5 6 7

Manufactured in the United States of America

ISBN: 978-0-87116-456-8
EISBN: 978-0-87116-754-5

Editor: Mary Wohlgemuth
Art Director: Lisa Bergman
Layout Designer: Lisa Schroeder
Photographers: James Forbes, William Zuback

Library of Congress Cataloging-in-Publication Data

Berlin, Kimberly Sciaraffa.
  Build your own wire pendants / Kimberly Sciaraffa Berlin.

   p. : col. ill. ; cm.

  Issued also as an ebook.
  "Choose a frame, make a bail, add embellishment"–Cover.
  ISBN: 978-0-87116-456-8

  1. Pendants (Jewelry)–Handbooks, manuals, etc. 2. Wire jewelry–Handbooks, manuals, etc.
  3. Jewelry making–Handbooks, manuals, etc. I. Title. II. Title: Wire pendants

TT212 .B47 2012
739.27

Contents

6   **How to Use This Book**

7   **Materials**

9   **Tools**

12   **Techniques & Embellishments**

19   **Framed Projects**
20   Raindrop Medley
23   Pharaoh's Pyramid
26   Circular Motion
29   Basic Twisted Frame
32   Side-looped Medley
35   Diamond Delight
38   Holiday Tree
41   Elongated Twisted Frame
44   Traditional Cross
48   Simply Red-hot Heart
51   Double Triangle Twisted Frame
54   Shining Star
57   Butterfly Dazzle
60   Contemporary Cross

63   **Drilled-bead Projects**
64   Big-bead Pendant
67   Front-drilled Pendant
70   Side-drilled Pendant

73   **Wire Bezel Projects**
74   Basic Wire Bezel
78   Upside-down Wire Bezel
81   Double-ended Wire Bezel
85   Bonus Finishing Techniques

95   **Resources**
      Acknowledgments
      From Kimberly

How to Use This Book

Build Your Own Wire Pendants is an easy-to-follow guide that introduces you to the joy of making unique pendants to enhance your jewelry designs. You'll develop your skills and, at the same time, you'll have fun making pendants. If you have never made a wire pendant before, I hope this book will inspire you to pick up some jewelry pliers and give it a try!

The first section briefs you on the basics of materials, tools, and techniques you will use to create the projects in this book. These techniques have been tested and demonstrated many times as I teach wirework classes, and this information will be an excellent reference as you work through the projects that follow. The techniques are interchangeable and can be used with almost any of the projects.

The projects included in this book are meant to be a jumping-off point for your creativity and offer you the opportunity to personalize all of your jewelry pieces. Each chapter is organized from beginner to advanced levels of challenge. You can create the pendants as shown or create your own variations by interchanging techniques and materials to take your pendant in a whole new direction.

I have also included a gallery of design options for each project to help illustrate how easy it is to adapt and modify any of the projects to suit your own color combinations and preferences. Whether you are a beginner or an experienced wire artist, I hope this book sets you on a path toward achieving your jewelry-making aspirations.

Kimberly Berlin

SAFETY BASICS

- Wear eye protection when working with metals and wire.
- When cutting wire, hold the wire end toward your work table. This will help to keep flying bits of wire to a minimum.
- Take periodic rest breaks to stretch.
- Use tools and chemicals according to the manufacturer's specifications.
- Work in a well-ventilated space.

Measurement conversions

Wire measurements are given in inches and fractional inches. The standard of measurement for beads is metric. To convert inches to millimeters, multiply by 25.4. To convert inches to centimeters, multiply by 2.54. Wire gauges given follow the American Wire Gauge system (also known as Brown & Sharpe); below is a chart that lists the gauge and the corresponding diameter in millimeters.

Gauge	Diameter
16-gauge	1.29mm
18-gauge	1.02mm
20-gauge	0.81mm
22-gauge	0.64mm
24-gauge	0.51mm
26-gauge	0.40mm
28-gauge	0.32mm
30-gauge	0.26mm

Materials

Just two kinds of materials are needed for your wirework pendant projects: a few types of wire and a small assortment of beads and cabochons.

Wire

Wire provides the structure for every project in this book. Wire is a wonderful, malleable material. You'll learn to manipulate it into shapes that range from nearly flat to fully dimensional.

Wire shape

Wire is fabricated into many shapes: round, half-round, square, triangular, twisted, and rectangular. For the projects in this book, you will use various gauges of round, square, and half-round wire.

Wire types

You can purchase many kinds of wire to use in your jewelry designs—gold, sterling silver, copper, brass, and various base metal mixtures. I recommend using either sterling silver (92.5% silver and 7.5% copper) or copper (99.9% copper) wire to make any of the projects in this book.

Sterling silver is a precious metal that is a dream to work with. The jewelry you make with sterling silver wire will wear beautifully and carry intrinsic value because of the metal. Copper is the softest and least expensive of the commonly available wires—it's a great starter wire. Copper is very workable; its properties are similar to sterling silver. I buy my copper wire by the pound from a jewelry supplier (and a pound goes a very long way).

Colored copper wire, usually called craft wire, is easy to find and makes a good practice wire as well. Fine-gauge colored wire can be used for sewing and edging details, but I don't recommend the heavier gauges for making pendant frames; the wire can't be hammered and manipulated in the same way that sterling silver or copper can.

As you shop for wire, you will see other options, such as filled or plated wire. Simply put, silver-filled or gold-filled wire

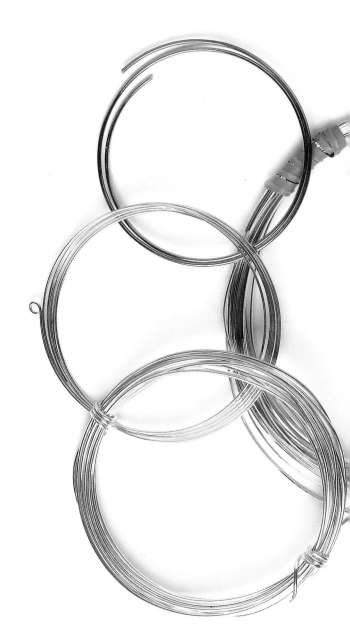

I look for a wide variety of one-of-a-kind cabochons to use in my wirework.

My tray of almost every shade of blue and green imaginable offers a variety of colors, shapes, and textures from which to choose.

contains more precious metal than the plated version. The filled versions are an economical option that can be used for making the Wire Bezel pendant projects in this book.

Wire temper

Temper refers to the hardness or malleability of the wire. There are three types of wire temper commonly available: dead-soft (often called simply "soft"), half-hard, and hard. Dead-soft wire is used for the projects in this book. The more you work with wire, the more it hardens, and it can eventually become brittle. This is called work-hardening.

Wire gauge

Wire comes in many different gauges. The gauge of the wire refers to the size or diameter of the wire, and the higher the number of the gauge, the thinner the wire. The projects in this book generally call for fairly thick 16- and 18-gauge wire that creates strong pendant frames to showcase your favorite beads. For finer work such as sewing with beads, you'll use much thinner wire, such as 24- and 26-gauge.

> TIP
> **Purchase wire in coils rather than on spools. Because it's not wound as tightly as spooled wire, coiled wire usually has fewer bends, curves, or other marks.**

Beads & cabochons

Costarring with wire in the pendants you create will be colorful beads and cabochons in all shapes and sizes.

Simply put, a bead is a stone, pearl, crystal, or other material that has a hole in it; a cabochon is a gemstone or other material that has a smooth face, a flat back, and no hole.

If you are like so many jewelry artists, your supply of beads seems to proliferate. One way to manage your assortment of leftovers, loose beads, findings, and gemstones is to organize them by color. This will help you develop palettes of color and texture from which to "audition" your bead assortments for each project.

Permanent marker

Tools

Purchase the highest-quality tools you can afford. It's helpful to try them out at a bead show or store to make sure they feel comfortable in your hands.

Basic toolkit

You'll need this setup for all of the pendant projects in this book. It is a versatile set of wireworking tools that will serve you well for a long time.

Permanent marker
Use a permanent marker, such as a fine-tipped Sharpie, to mark measurements on wire. Marks can be removed with a polishing cloth or as the piece is polished in a rotary tumbler.

Flush wire cutters
Flush cutters are used to cut wire so the ends are nearly flat. This simplifies filing and helps eliminate burs—tiny, rough projections on metal that can catch on clothing. Wire cutters have two sides: one flat and one angled. Cutting with the flat side of the cutter against your work creates a flush cut. When cutting wire, you'll usually place the angled side of the cutter toward the waste end. You will need a good pair of flush cutters that will allow you to easily cut wire up to 16-gauge.

Chainnose pliers
Chainnose pliers (sometimes referred to as needlenose pliers) have jaws that taper to a narrow point. The jaws are flat on the inner surface and curved on the outer surface. They come in many lengths and widths. Use these pliers for sewing wire, pulling, and getting at hard-to-reach spots within your work.

Flatnose pliers
Flatnose pliers are used to open and close jump rings, create sharp bends in wire, and hold wire steady as it is manipulated. The jaws of these pliers are wide and flat where they meet.

Nylon-jaw pliers
Use nylon-jaw pliers to straighten small, unwanted bends or curves in your wire. Nylon-jaw pliers are gentle on the wire and will not mar it like metal pliers can.

Flush wire cutters

Chainnose pliers

Flatnose pliers

Nylon-jaw pliers

Roundnose pliers

Bail-making pliers

Files and wire rounder

Bench block

Chasing hammer

Painters tape

Roundnose pliers

Roundnose pliers have long, conical jaws and are used for making loops and curves. For wirework, roundnose pliers with jaws that are 1½" long offer many positions at which to form the wire; the closer to the tip of the jaw, the smaller the loop.

> **TIP**
>
> **Mark roundnose pliers with a permanent marker to guide your wirework. Starting at the tips, mark every ¼" on both jaws. By working at the same mark, you will be able to duplicate loop and curve sizes when making more than one of an item.**

Bail-making pliers

These pliers have jaws with different diameters, allowing you make loops, small quantities of jump rings, and bails in two sizes. The pliers shown have jaws that are 7mm and 9mm in diameter.

Files and wire rounder

Use small files or a wire rounder to smooth the ends of wire and clean up burs after the wire has been trimmed. File with an upward stroke only.

Bench block

A bench block is a smooth piece of hardened stainless steel that is used as a surface for hammering metals. Bench blocks come in different sizes. A 4" square bench block is adequate for making most jewelry projects. To flatten wire on a bench block, place the wire on the block and strike it repeatedly with the flat face of the hammer.

Chasing hammer

This hammer, although originally designed to strike chasing tools and stamps, has been adopted by many wireworkers. The chasing hammer has one large circular, slightly convex face and a balled end opposite. The slightly convex face works well for flattening, tapering, and hardening wire. The balled end can be used for texturing.

Ruler

Texture hammer

Ball-peen hammer

Ruler
I use a ruler with imperial (inch) and metric markings and a deep center tray. Place the wire in the tray to measure it.

Safety glasses
Wear safety glasses to protect your eyes from wire cuttings and other debris.

Polishing cloth
Give your pendants a final shine with this soft cloth that has a special polishing agent embedded in it.

Optional items
Some of these items are called for in only a few projects, and some are not absolutely necessary but may be helpful as you continue your journey in wireworking.

Painters tape
Easy-release, nonresidue painters tape is a staple in my method for wrapping cabochons. It's needed for projects in the last section of this book, which focuses on wire-wrapped pendant ideas. Use tape that is ³⁄₄" wide.

Texture hammer
A texture hammer is used to make decorative marks as you hammer the wire. There are many different types of texture hammers on the market.

Ball-peen hammer
A ball-peen hammer has one flat face and a balled end opposite. You can flatten and spread wire with the flat end and texture the wire with the balled end.

TIP
When hammering to flatten and smooth wire, make sure that the hammer and the bench block have no scratches or nicks, which can transfer as unwanted texture to metal. As you strike the wire, you will work-harden it, strengthening the shape.

Visor-style magnifiers
Wearing an Opti-visor or other magnifying glasses reduces eye strain and helps you see small imperfections so that you can more easily fix them.

Tumbler
A rotary or vibrating tumbler can be used to remove light scratches, clean, and add luster to most metals. Use the tumbler about one third full of mixed-media stainless steel shot, add a drop of baby shampoo, and add water to cover the shot and pieces you are tumbling. Tumbling time varies according to the materials to be tumbled (anywhere from about 20 minutes to 2 hours).

Rotary tumbler

Techniques & Embellishments

The techniques and embellishments explained in these pages will help you build and enhance your designs. They can be interchanged and adapted from project to project. Enjoy using them to add personality and dimension to every pendant you create. As you work through the projects, refer back to these instructions.

Loops, spirals, and jump rings

Opening jump rings and making simple loops, eye loops, wrapped loops, double-wrapped loops, and spirals are some of the basic skills necessary to complete your pendant projects. These basic instructions should give you a grasp of these skills.

Simple loop

Holding the roundnose pliers on a flat plain, place the wire between the jaws at the ¼" mark **[a]**. You should barely feel the tip of the wire sticking out of the top of the pliers. The longest portion of wire should extend from the bottom of the pliers. Keeping the pliers flat, grab the longest piece of the wire with your fingers while slightly rolling the pliers toward you. Pull the wire toward your chest and over the top of the pliers. Stop when the wire is flat across the top of the pliers **[b]**. Remove the wire from the pliers **[c]**.

Eye loop

With chainnose pliers, make a 90-degree bend in the wire just above a bead **[a]**. Next, grasp the wire at the bend with roundnose pliers and roll the wire in the opposite direction of the bend to form a circular loop **[b]**. Trim any excess wire **[c]**. The finished loop should be a perfect circle **[d]**. Open an eye loop just as you would a jump ring.

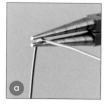 

Wrapped loop

With flatnose pliers, make a 90-degree bend in the wire at least 2" from the end of the wire. Grasp the wire at the bend with roundnose pliers **[a]**. With your fingers, pull the wire over the top jaw of the pliers and roll the pliers to make a complete centered loop **[b]**. Grasp the loop with flatnose pliers and use chainnose pliers to wrap the tail of the wire around the neck of the wire **[c]**. Make the wraps close and tight. Trim any excess wire and use chainnose pliers to tuck the wire tail against the base wire **[d]**.

Double-wrapped loop

Make a wrapped loop at one end of the wire, string a bead, and make a 90-degree bend ¹⁄₁₆" over the bead. Follow the steps shown in **a–d** of "Wrapped loop" to complete the loop.

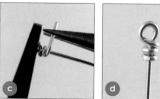

Opening and closing a jump ring

Using two pairs of flatnose pliers (or one flatnose and one chainnose), grasp the jump ring on both sides of the join (cut). Open the jump ring by pushing gently and moving one end up and the other down. To close the jump ring, use the same pushing motion and move the ends toward each other. You should hear a faint click when the ends align perfectly and the jump ring is tightly closed.

Spiral

To start a spiral, squeeze the wire end with flatnose pliers. Make a simple loop at the slightly flattened end of the wire with the roundnose pliers **[a]**. Using roundnose or chainnose pliers, continue shaping the wire to start a second loop around the first **[b]**. Hold the spiral with flatnose pliers and turn it while guiding the wire around with your fingers, pushing the wire around and against the previous spiral **[c]**. Repeat this step by regripping the spiral and shaping the wire in small movements until the spiral is complete.

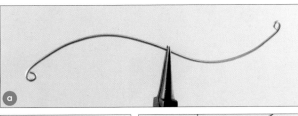

Flush-cutting wire and smoothing the end

Trim the wire with the flat side of the cutter toward the work and the angled side toward the waste end to create a flush cut **[a]**. Smooth the end using a small file with upward strokes **[b]** or rotate a cup bur several times around the end.

S-curve spiral component

To make an S-curve spiral with a finished length of about 1¼", flush-cut 8" of wire and mark the center with permanent marker. Using roundnose pliers, make a simple loop at one end and another loop at the opposite end facing the opposite direction. Using your fingers, make a gentle curve on each end following the curve of each loop **[a]**. This curve should help make the spiraling action go smoothly. Make a spiral on one side of the wire, stopping at the center mark **[b]**. Make

a second spiral in the opposite direction, also stopping at the center mark. The spirals should end up against each other **[c]**.

Wrapped spiral component

After you make the end loops and curve the wire following the steps above, wrap the base wire with 24- or 26-gauge wire **[d]** and then spiral each wrapped end as described above **[e]**.

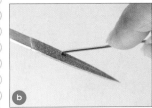

Bails

The bail is at the top of a pendant. It's usually a loop of some sort that allows the pendant to slide over a chain or attach to a beaded necklace or other form of neckwire. By using one of the bails shown here, you'll be able to move a pendant from one necklace to another.

Wrapped-loop bail

A wrapped-loop bail is often used with a drilled stone or bead. To make a wrapped-loop bail, follow the directions for making a wrapped loop (p. 12), but instead of using the roundnose pliers to create the loop, form it on one of the barrels of the bail-making pliers. In this way, you can create smaller or larger bails to fit your needs. If necessary, use flatnose pliers to twist the bail so it is perpendicular to the pendant.

Half-round bail

Cut 3" of 10- or 12-gauge half-round wire. Trim one end with the angled side of the flush cutter to create a beveled edge. File the bevel smooth. With roundnose pliers, make a simple loop at this end, making sure the flat side of the wire is on the inside of the loop and the curved side faces out. Do not close this loop completely yet. Slide the pendant onto the looped end and finish closing the loop **[a]**. The pendant front should face the same direction as this loop. With the bail-making pliers, make a larger loop over the previous loop (I used the smaller jaw of the pliers). The curved side of the new top loop should face out and should be oriented in the same direction as the first loop **[b]**. Make a beveled cut on the end of the wire, even with the small loop **[c]**. File the end smooth. Close the large loop completely **[d]**.

Spiral with half-round bail

Bend the wire at a 90-degree angle over the pendant **[a]**. Make a simple loop on the end of the wire and continue spiraling until the spiral meets the bead (see p. 13) **[b]**. Place the spiral on the bench block and hammer it with the wide face of the chasing hammer to flatten it slightly and harden it **[c]**. Attach a half-round bail to the top of the spiral **[d]**.

Over-under bail

Cut 3" of 10- or 12-gauge half-round wire. Trim one end with the angled side of the flush cutter to create a bevel on the end **[a]**. File the end smooth. With roundnose pliers, make a simple loop at this end, making sure the flat side of the wire is inside and the curved side faces out **[b]**. Before you close the loop completely, slide a pendant onto the looped end with the loop closure at the back. Finish closing the loop **[c]**. With bail-making pliers, make a larger loop above the simple loop. This new loop should face the opposite direction of the first loop, and the flat side of the wire will face out **[d]**. Make another beveled cut with the flush cutters on this end of the wire and file smooth. Then close the loop completely **[e]**.

TIP
You can also use 12-gauge round wire for this bail.

Spring bail

Tightly wrap 18-gauge round wire four times around one barrel of the bail-making pliers **[a]**. Slide the wire off and trim the ends flush by placing the flat side of the cutters toward the coil of wire (the angled side will face the end to be trimmed away) **[b, c]**. Smooth any burs or sharp edges with a file. Feed the spring bail directly onto a pendant, eye loop, or wrapped loop in the same way you would attach a key to a key ring.

Eye loop over-under bail

Using the wire at the top of the pendant, make a small eye loop. Then make an over-under bail and attach it to the eye loop.

Wrapped loop half-round bail

Using the wire at the top of the pendant, make a small wrapped loop. Then make a small half-round bail and attach it to the eye loop.

Fine-gauge wire techniques

These techniques allow you to embellish, strengthen, and add dimension to projects using fine 24- or 26-gauge wire.

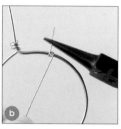

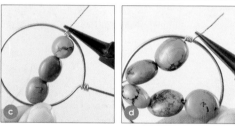

Sewing

Flush cut 4–12" of 24- or 26-gauge round wire. With chainnose pliers, make a 45-degree bend 1" from one end **[a]**. This end is the wire tail you will hold in the pliers as you wrap the other end around the frame with your fingers. Place the wire bend over the frame and make at least three tight wraps around the frame with the other end **[b]**. String beads or stones on the fine-gauge wire. Then wrap the wire to another place on the frame, making at least three wraps **[c]**. If you have more wire to work with and more space on the frame, continue to sew in beads until the design is complete **[d]**. Trim the excess wire and bend and tuck the end against the frame wire.

Edging

Edging a section or a whole piece is similar to sewing with wire. Start with at least 8" of 24 or 26-gauge round wire. Make a small bend about ½" from one end of the wire. Hook the bend at the spot where you want the edging to begin. Holding the tail of the bend in chainnose pliers, use your fingers to wrap the longer end of the wire at least three times around the frame. String a small bead onto the wire **[a]**. Slide the bead about ½" up the wire and bend over the bead **[b]**. With your fingers, press the wire together below the bead and twist it several times while holding the bead **[c]**. Make at least two wraps on the frame where you will continue to edge in the same way **[d]**.

TIP

If you want longer twists, try sliding the bead ⅝" up the wire instead of to the ½" point. Increase in increments of ⅛" until the twist is the desired length.

▲ The freshwater pearl edging accentuates the large pearl focal bead in this Circular Motion pendant.

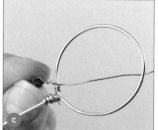

Supports and tightening

You may need to add supports for strength to some frames. You'll usually do this on the back of the frame, but you can also add supports to the front in a more decorative way to divide different colors or textures of beads or stones. To add supports, cut a piece of 20-gauge round wire at least 3" longer than the diameter of the frame. At one end of the wire, make a hook. Place the hook on the frame where you want the support to begin. Make at least three tight wraps around the frame, making sure the wraps are very close together **[a]**. Place the other end of the wire where you want the support to end and wrap at least three times around the frame **[b]**. Repeat this process as many times as needed. To tighten a support, you can add bends or kinks in the support by grasping with flatnose pliers and rotating the pliers a bit **[c]**. Bends can be placed strategically to add design and texture to your pendant.

◀ In this pendant, the supports stabilize the geode slice in the frame.

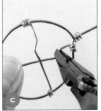

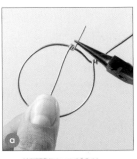

Large wire accents

Adding large wire accents with thick, 16- or 18-gauge round wire gives a pendant dimension and can frame beads you want to emphasize. Flush-cut a length of wire approximately double the diameter of the pendant. File the ends to remove any burs. Make a small bend in one end of the wire and hook it at the point in the frame where you want the accent to begin. Wrap the wire at least two times around the frame **[a]**. Using your fingers or roundnose pliers, make simple loops in the wire over and around beads you want to accent **[b]**. Attach the end of the wire to the frame **[c]**. Trim excess wire with flush cutters and file the end smooth.

TIP
Use more wire to add more accents and create bolder designs.

▲ The large wire accent not only adds texture to this pendant, but it also adds support to the glass cabochon.

▲ Green crystal beads are highlighted by the large wire accent.

▲ The large wire accent ties the design together and adds dimension.

Finishing techniques

Add dimension and character to your pieces by texturing them with a hammer and adding patina to accentuate the details.

Flattening and texturing with a hammer

Place your bench block on a piece of smooth cloth, so that when you hammer, you keep the force of the strike in the block and you reduce the noise factor. A doubled piece of old polishing cloth works great.

Use the wide face of the chasing hammer to flatten, harden, and create a smooth finish on the wire. Use the balled end of the hammer to create texture. By focusing on where you are hammering, you can be very specific about which areas become textured. Enhance the texture of a piece by adding a patina, such as liver of sulfur, which will stay in the low spots of the texture.

Adding patina

Applying a solution of liver of sulfur is a common, safe way to add an antique finish to wire. It is nontoxic but very stinky. Use it in a well-ventilated area and follow the manufacturer's directions. Liver of sulfur is available as dry chunks, to which you add water, or as a ready-to-use liquid or gel (I like the gel). You won't use much of any of these forms to add patina to a small project. Each application will produce slightly different results and colorations, so for the best results, use the same batch to add patina to all the parts of each project.

Notes on designing

Your frame design choice will usually guide your choice of the stones, beads, glass, or crystals used to embellish your pendant. However, it can work in reverse: Your choice of materials can also dictate the choice of frame.

Many times I find a particular lampwork bead or small stone that I just love. I look at its shape and decide which frame type would best support its form and which complementary beads I should incorporate with it.

After I shape a frame, I place it on my work table and position my cabochon and beads within it. I move things around to create an arrangement I like before I attach any elements with wire. Sometimes I add or subtract beads from the frame. I think of this as "auditioning" the beads. Try this process as you make your pendants.

Keep in mind that you do not have to fill in every space in a frame; open space can add interest to your work.

◀ *This lovely deep-green drusy suggested the frame type I created and the accent beads I used.*

Creating small sets of beads and cabochons that show a variety of colors, textures, sizes, and shapes helps me generate new ideas.

Build Your Own
Framed Projects

Showcase your favorite cabochons and beads in 14 distinct frame designs. Create the pendants as presented or have fun customizing them with variations of the bails and embellishments you add.

In this simple, elegant Elongated Twisted Frame, I combined a natural agate drusy and a variety of freshwater pearls. See p. 41 to learn how to create this style of frame.

Raindrop Medley

The teardrop shape of this pendant draws the eye from the wearer's collarbone to the pendant. Many kinds of stones and beads work well with this shape.

MATERIALS

Wire:
- **10"** 16-gauge round (frame)
- **3"** 12-gauge half-round (bail)
- **3–6'** 24- or 26-gauge round (sewing)
- **10"** 18-gauge round (accent)

Bead assortment such as:
- **3** 10mm turquoise tube beads
- **17** 6mm turquoise beads
- **16** 4mm turquoise beads
- **2** 3mm turquoise beads
- **3** 6mm onyx beads
- **20** 3mm onyx beads
- **6** 4mm onyx beads
- **6** 2mm sterling silver beads

Finished length: 3½"

Frame

Flush-cut a 10" piece of 16-gauge round wire and smooth the ends. With permanent marker, mark the center of the wire. Cross the ends of the wire to create a gently curved teardrop shape **[a]**.

With flatnose pliers, bend one end to point upward and bend the other end at a right angle to the first **[b]**.

Bring the two bends together so they touch and, using chainnose pliers, wrap the end that has a right angle twice around the wire that is pointing straight up **[c]**. Flush-cut the excess wire from the wrapping wire. File and tuck the end in.

Bail

Make an eye-loop half-round bail **[d, e]**. Using the chasing hammer and the bench block, work-harden and flatten the entire frame except the wrapped neck **[f]**.

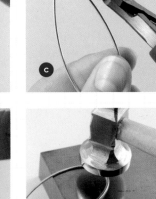

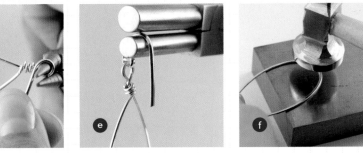

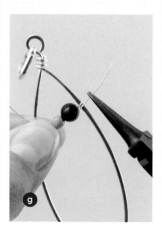

Embellishment

Choose your bead assortment and audition the beads in the frame. I used a variety of sizes of turquoise beads, onyx beads, and silver balls.

Using short lengths (4–10") of the 24- or 26-gauge round wire, sew in the components **[g, h]**. Wrap each piece of wire three to five times after each group of beads. After sewing in your beads, sew in a large wire accent (see p. 17) made with 18-gauge wire **[i]**.

design
options

This pendant is designed around a geode slice. Because the geode is a dramatic focal point, I didn't need a large wire accent.

◀ I love the orange and lime-green color palette of the square glass bead, so I combined it with a supporting cast of matching lampwork beads, natural stone, and pearls.

This pendant has a lot of depth. It incorporates a natural stone bead, a complementary flat lampwork disk, garnets, and pearls. ▶

Pharaoh's Pyramid

This is a very versatile frame that can be easily manipulated to suit your needs. For example, by enlarging it just a bit, the same frame can easily accommodate larger beads and stones for a very dramatic look.

MATERIALS

Wire:
- **6"** 16-gauge round (frame)
- **3"** 10-gauge half-round (bail)
- **5–10'** 24- or 26-gauge round (sewing)

Bead assortment such as:
- 10mm coin pearl
- **2** 5mm freshwater pearls
- **2** 4mm fresh water pearls
- 2mm freshwater pearl
- **4** 2mm sterling silver beads
- **30** size 6 and size 8 mixed-color seed beads

Finished length: 2"

Frame

Flush-cut 6" of 16-gauge round wire. Smooth the ends.

With permanent marker, mark the center of the wire. Make a mark ½" from the center mark on each side **[a]**. With flatnose pliers, make

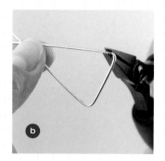

90-degree angle bends at the ½" marks so both wires point up. Push the wires together so they cross each other **[b]**.

TIP

These directions make a triangle with 1" sides. If you want to change the size of the frame, draw a pattern on a piece of paper and use the drawing as a guide to help you position the bends and the point where the wires cross.

With flatnose pliers, bend one end so it is at a right angle to the other **[c]**.

With chainnose pliers, wrap the bent wire at least two times around the straight wire **[d]**. Trim the excess wire and smooth any burs. Make an eye loop with the remaining wire **[e]**.

Bail

With the 10-gauge half-round wire, make a half-round top bail and place it through the eye loop **[f]**.

Using the chasing hammer and the bench block, work-harden and flatten the entire frame except the wrapped neck **[g]**.

Embellishment

Choose your bead assortment and audition the beads in the frame. I used a variety of seed beads in various colors, pearls, and sterling silver beads.

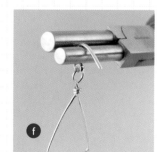

Using short (4–10") lengths of the 24- or 26-gauge wire, begin sewing in the beads **[h, i]**, making three to five wraps for each sewn-in bead **[j]**.

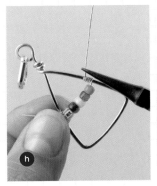

design options

A long black tourmaline crystal carries one side of this pendant. A turquoise bead and round black garnet beads give this pendant a classic look. The large wire accent highlights the garnet beads and ties the pendant together.

◀ Make a smaller triangular base with elongated sides for a longer drop pendant.

To showcase this large ▶ focal geode slice, I used more wire to create a larger frame. I also used support wire across the front of the stone.

Circular Motion

You can create simple, elegant pendants with this frame.
It lends itself to a wide variety of stone and bead choices and can
be made large or small to suit your purpose.

MATERIALS
- 1½"-diameter pill bottle for a mandrel

Wire:
- **12"** 16-gauge round (frame)
- **8"** 16-gauge round (spiral component)
- **2'** 24-gauge round (wrapping)
- **3–6'** 24- or 26-gauge round (sewing)

Bead assortment such as:
- **18mm** carnelian tube bead
- **5** 8mm round faceted carnelian beads
- **3** 2mm carnelian beads
- **20** 3mm copper hexagonal beads
- **10** 3mm pale yellow faceted rondelles
- **12** 2mm copper beads

Finished length: 2¼"

Frame

Flush-cut 12" of 16-gauge round wire and smooth the ends. With permanent marker, mark the center of the wire. Place the wire against the pill bottle mandrel with the center mark at the bottom of the mandrel.

Wrap the wire around the mandrel so the ends cross each other at the top **[a]**. With flatnose pliers, bend one end straight up **[b]**.

Grasp the other end with chainnose pliers and tightly wrap it twice around the end that's pointing up **[c]**. (Don't trim the excess wire; you can use it in your design.)

Slide the circular frame off the mandrel. Hammer the circular portion of the pendant only **[d]**.

Bail

Make a wrapped-loop bail with one wire end, incorporating the remaining wire end into the design by draping it across the frame and attaching it to the side **[e]**. Add edging to this wire before you sew in any other components **[f]**. (If you want to use a different bail style, trim the extra wire, smooth the end, and tuck it in.)

Embellishment

Choose your bead assortment and audition the beads in the frame. I used carnelian and copper beads with a wrapped S-curve spiral component (p. 13). Using short lengths (4–10") of the 24- or 26-gauge wire, sew in the beads and the spiral component **[g, h]**.

design options

The Circular Motion frame allows for a dramatic change in pendant size. Consider using less wire to create a delicate pendant with small bead embellishments.

This alternative uses a cool color palette. I also changed the positions of the elements within the frame.

For a simple, beautiful pendant, I used the wire edging technique to emphasize a large freshwater coin pearl.

This version uses fairly monochromatic colors of stone beads and pearls. The spiral component brings the eye to specific beads.

Basic Twisted Frame

The Basic Twisted Frame is very versatile and can be manipulated easily to fit a variety of beads, stones, and findings. Simply use more wire and enlarge the looped curves to incorporate larger elements for a bold, dramatic statement.

MATERIALS

Wire:
- **7"** 16-gauge round (frame)
- **3"** 12-gauge half-round (bail)
- **4–8'** 24- or 26-gauge round (sewing)

Bead assortment such as:
- 4x15mm glass tube bead
- 10mm round bead
- **6** 4mm pearls
- 4mm round crystal bead
- 3mm bicone crystal beads
- **5** 3mm bicone beads
- **2** 3mm copper beads
- **12** 2mm copper beads

Finished length: 1⅞"

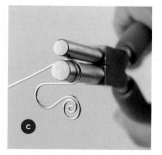

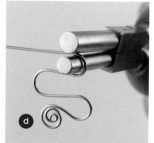

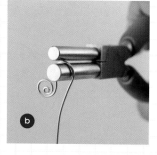

Frame

Flush-cut 7" of 16-gauge round wire. Smooth the ends.

With roundnose pliers, make a simple loop and a small open spiral on one end of the wire. Spiral at least two full times around **[a]**.

Make a curve over the large jaw of the bail-making pliers as shown **[b]**.

Make another curve over the large jaw as shown **[c]**.

Over the small jaw, make a curve as shown **[d]**.

Make another simple loop and a small open spiral on the other end of the wire for the bottom of the pendant **[e]**.

Push all the curves together so they touch **[f]**. If the spirals are not centered, spiral each shape a little more to center it.

Using the chasing hammer and the bench block, work-harden and flatten the entire frame **[g]**.

Bail

Using 12-gauge half-round wire, make an over-under bail and attach it to the top of the spiral.

Embellishment

Choose your bead assortment and audition the beads in the frame. I used a variety of glass beads, lampwork beads, crystals, pearls, and copper findings. Using short lengths (4–10") of the 24- or 26-gauge wire, sew in the beads, starting with the tube and large glass bead **[h]**. Then sew in the remainder of the beads **[i, j]**.

design
options

▲ This Basic Twisted Frame incorporates a green turquoise cabochon and a matching lampwork bead for emphasis. The large accent wire highlights the lampwork bead.

▲ For this formal black-and-white design, I chose a small rutilated quartz cabochon, a lampwork bead, and onyx accent beads.

Consider using the large wire accent technique with this frame style. I made large overlapping loops down the center of this pendant.

▲ A rough-cut gold rutilated quartz cabochon mixed with tourmaline is stunning. I formed a sunburst detail over the cabochon using the support wire technique and added a large wire accent along the side to emphasize the tourmaline beads.

▲ I framed a pretty pink rhodochrosite bead with pearls.

▲ A beautiful freshwater pearl is the focal point of this amethyst bead pendant. I encircled the pearl with a large wire accent.

◀ I found an oblong piece of charoite at a bead show and simply had to frame it to show it off. Instead of just looping the large wire accent, I created strategic bends in the wire over the gemstone.

Side-looped Medley

Strategically placed loops highlight certain beads in this frame.
To change the design and accommodate beads of different sizes, you can
vary loop sizes or even place loops outside the frame.

MATERIALS
- 5 16-gauge 10mm closed
  jump rings

Wire:
- **10"** 16-gauge round (frame)
- **3"** 12-gauge half-round (bail)
- **5–10'** 24- or 26-gauge
  round (sewing)

Turquoise bead assortment
  such as:
- 12mm rondelle
- 2 8mm round beads
- 4mm round bead
- 3 2mm round beads
- 5 3mm beads

Additional beads:
- 3 8mm glass donuts

Finished length: 2³⁄₄"

TIP
To help shape the frame, you can draw a pattern on paper and use it as a template to make sure your curves and bends are aligned and the wire ends cross each other correctly.

Frame
Flush-cut 10" of 16-gauge round wire. Smooth the ends.

With permanent marker, mark 1¼" from one end of the wire. Make another mark 2" from the other end.

Using flatnose pliers, make a 90-degree bend at the 2" mark **[a]**. The direction the wire end is pointing establishes the outside of the shape.

Below the bend, make two more marks at 2" intervals. Working near the base of the roundnose pliers jaws or using the small jaw of the bail-making pliers, make a large (10mm) loop facing in at each of the two marks as shown **[b]**.

With your fingers, shape the wire into a 1½"-diameter circle with the loops on the inside. The wire ends should cross each other **[c]**.

Use flatnose pliers to bend the straight end 90 degrees as shown **[d]**.

Grasp the wire that is extended toward the side of the pendant with chainnose pliers and wrap it at least two times around the wire that's pointed up. Trim the excess wrapping wire and smooth the end.

With the remaining wire, make an open spiral **[e]** .

Using the chasing hammer and the bench block, work-harden and flatten the entire frame except the wrapped neck and in the loops where the wire crosses itself **[f]**.

Bail
With the 12-gauge wire, make a half-round bail and place it through the spiral **[g]**.

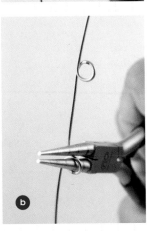

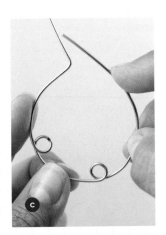

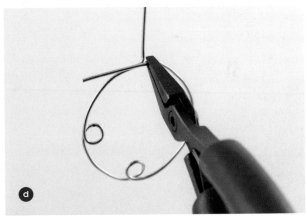

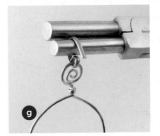

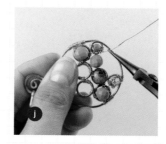

Embellishment

Choose your bead assortment and audition the beads in the frame. I used a variety of complementary glass beads, turquoise rounds and rondelles, and closed jump rings.

Using short (4–10") lengths of 24- or 26-gauge wire, sew in the jump rings, anchoring the first ring to one of the loops in the frame and another point on the frame **[h]**. Wrap three times around to anchor the sewing wire, then wrap three to five times to connect the ring to the anchor point, and make three wraps around the ring to finish. Continue in the same way to connect rings to each other **[i]**.

After sewing in your jump rings, begin sewing in beads **[j]**. Use wire supports or wire accents as needed **[k]**.

design options

Sea agate disk beads are the focal point in this pendant. I created an attached spring bail from one of the frame's wire ends.

▲ Use closed jump rings to encircle the Side-looped Medley pendant. Highlight three focal beads by sewing them into the center loops.

▲ Use the wire-and-bead edging technique to create an eye-catching pendant. I sewed different sizes of pearls and stone beads into the center loops.

Diamond Delight

This is an elegant, symmetrical design. Dramatically modify the look by choosing a wilder mix of crystals or beads, rotating the positions of the circles, or adding edging to the outside of the frame. The pendant can take on a whimsical or classical personality based on your choices.

MATERIALS
- 5 10mm closed jump rings

Wire:
- 8" 16-gauge round (frame)
- 3–6' 26-gauge round (sewing)

Bead assortment such as:
- 4 8mm round crystals
- 8mm pearl

Finished length: 2"

Frame
Flush-cut 8" of 16-gauge round wire. Smooth the ends.

With the permanent marker, mark the center of the wire and make a 90-degree bend at that point **[a]**. This will be the bottom of the pendant.

Mark 1" on each side of the bend. Using flatnose pliers, make a 90-degree bend in each end so the ends face each other **[b]**.

At the top of the frame where the wires cross, use chainnose pliers to bend one end so it points straight up **[c]**. Wrap the other end at least three times around the bend in the end

pointing up. Trim the excess wire and smooth the ends. Using the chasing hammer and the bench block, work-harden and flatten the entire frame except the wrapped neck.

Bail
Make a wrapped-loop bail **[d]**.

Embellishment
Choose your bead assortment and audition the beads in the frame. I used jump rings, crystals, and a pearl. Use the 26-gauge wire to sew the jump rings to each other, placing a jump ring in each corner and one in the center **[e]**. They will be arranged in a cross shape in the frame.

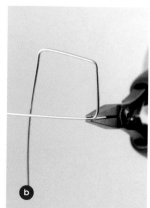

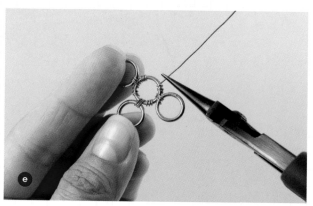

Place the jump-ring centerpiece into the frame and sew it to the frame **[f]**.

Sew in the center pearl. Sew a crystal in each of the four remaining jump ring centers **[g]**.

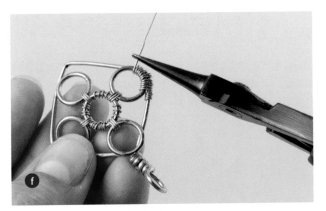

design
options

▲ Here's a version with delicate detailing: Edge with pearls and crystals to echo the large center pearl and large crystals.

▲ Colored crystals create a festive look.

Go bold: I centered an agate slice that had a large open space (an agate donut!). I used the large wire accent technique to highlight a pearl as though it were floating through the hole.

Holiday Tree

This holiday tree pendant is beautiful in a traditional color palette of greens and reds. Or, express your whimsy by choosing a nontraditional mix of colors and materials.

MATERIALS

Wire:
- **8"** 16-gauge round (frame)
- **3"** 12-gauge half-round (bail)
- **5–10'** 24- or 26-gauge (sewing)
- **10"** 18-gauge round (wire accent)
- **10"** 20-gauge round (supports; optional)

Bead assortment such as:
- **4** 8mm round lime-green beads
- **8–10** 6mm bicone crystals (turquoise a/b)
- **2** 5mm Czech fire-polished beads (brown)
- **16–20** 4mm bicone crystals (turquoise a/b)
- **18–20** size 8 lime-green seed beads

Finished length: 2¾"

Frame

Flush-cut 8" of 16-gauge round wire. Smooth the ends.

With the permanent marker, mark the wire 3½" from one end. Make two more marks, each ⅛" from each side of the first mark. You may find it helpful to make a template as a guide for marking the wire **[a]**. With flatnose pliers, make 90-degree bends at the ⅛" marks so both ends point up to form the tree trunk **[b]**.

Make two more 90-degree bends ⅛" from each bend as shown **[c, d]**. The new bends are the bottom bough of the tree.

Make a 90-degree bend ¾" from each of the last two bends to form the sides of the tree **[e]**.

Using your fingers, gently push the wires so they cross.

Measuring from the shorter end, mark the 1" point. Measuring from the longer end, mark the 2" point. These marks show where the ends will cross to form the peak of the tree **[f]**.

Use flatnose pliers to bend the ends at the marks so they are perpendicular to each other as shown, with the short end pointing to the side **[g]**.

Make an open spiral with the longer wire end. With chainnose pliers, wrap the short end around the base of the spiral. Trim the excess wrapping wire and smooth any burs.

Using the chasing hammer and the bench block, work-harden and flatten the entire frame except the wrapped neck.

Bail

Use the 12-gauge wire to make a half-round bail. Attach it to the top of the spiral **[h]**.

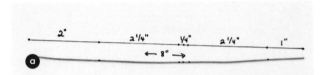

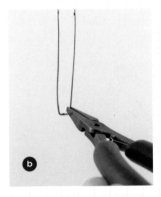

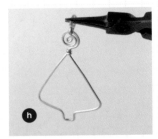

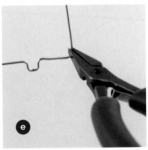

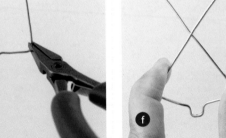

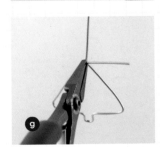

 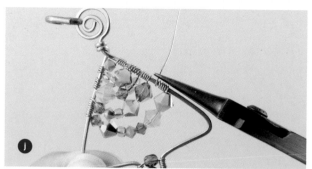 

Embellishment

Choose your bead assortment and audition the beads in the frame. I used a variety of seed beads, crystals, and glass beads in random order within this frame.

Using short (4–7") lengths of 24- or 26-gauge wire, sew in the beads **[i, j]**. Make three to five wraps for each bead or strand of beads. Sew in a large wire accent (p. 17). I wanted to emphasize the large lime-green glass beads, so I used the large wire accent to encircle each of them **[k]**.

design options

▲ This option features monochromatic colors of copper and a large wire accent. The varied copper tones look lovely worn over a simple black blouse or dress.

▲ Curve 16-gauge wire with roundnose pliers to make a tree shape that matches the frame shape. Hammer it flat, sew it to the frame, and sew in some crystals.

▲ This variation shows off traditional Christmas colors. I skipped the large wire accent.

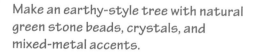

Make an earthy-style tree with natural green stone beads, crystals, and mixed-metal accents.

Elongated Twisted Frame

This eye-catching, asymmetrical shape is ideal for displaying long cabochons, beads, or glass.

MATERIALS
Wire:
- **10"** 16-gauge round (frame)
- **6",** 18-gauge round (bail)
- **6–10'** 24- or 26-gauge round (sewing)
- **12"** 18-gauge round (accent)

Bead assortment such as:
- **2** 12mm tube beads
- **2** 8mm glass beads
- 8mm freshwater pearl
- 6mm copper bead
- **2** 4mm round crystals
- **4** 3mm copper beads
- **2** 3mm agate beads
- **20** 2mm round crystals

Finished length: 2"

Frame

Flush-cut 10" of 16-gauge round wire. Smooth the ends.

With roundnose pliers, make a simple loop at one end of the wire. Make a spiral, spiraling around at least two complete turns **[a]**. The spiral will become the top of the pendant.

With permanent marker, mark ½" from the spiral. With flatnose pliers, make a soft 90-degree bend in the wire at the mark **[b]**.

Mark 1⅛" from the last bend. Use bail-making pliers to grasp the wire at the mark. Rotate the jaws to make a bend as shown, so the end points up toward the spiral **[c]**.

Grasp the end with flatnose pliers at the point where it crosses the spiral. Make a 90-degree bend as shown **[d]**.

Make three curves that run along the side of the long shape: Make the first curve around the small jaw of the bail-making pliers **[e]**. Use roundnose pliers to make the second curve **[f]**. Make the third curve around the small jaw of the bail-making pliers **[g]**.

With roundnose pliers, make a spiral at the end of the wire **[h]**. This is the bottom of the pendant.

Manipulate the loops so they touch the side of the large shape. Using the chasing hammer and the bench block, work-harden and flatten the entire frame. Use your fingers to reshape the frame after hammering.

Bail

Use the 18-gauge wire to make a spring bail and attach it to the top spiral.

Embellishment

Choose your bead assortment and audition the beads in the frame. I used agate tube beads, copper beads of various sizes, a chocolate pearl, crystals, a lampwork bead, and vintage German glass beads. In place of the tube beads, you could use a single long bead.

Using short (4–10") lengths of 24- or 26-gauge wire, begin sewing in the beads. Sew a long bead into the long shape first (I strung two tube beads for this space) **[i]**. Make three to five wraps for each sewn-in bead.

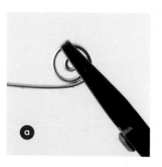
a

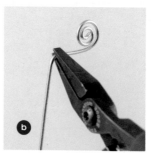
b

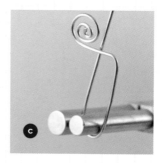
c

d

e

f

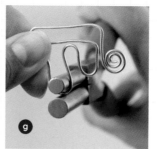
g

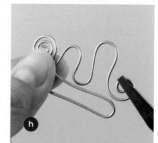
h

Continue sewing to fill the frame as desired **[j]**. Sew in a large accent wire encircling the beads you want to highlight, wrapping the long bead(s) three times **[k]**.

design options

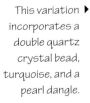

This variation ▶ incorporates a double quartz crystal bead, turquoise, and a pearl dangle.

▲ Consider flipping the frame and placing the long bead on the opposite side.

◀ I found this long variscite cabochon at a rock and mineral show. I angled it in the frame to show it off and added a lampwork bead in lime green and black to tie in the onyx beads.

I flipped the frame and made wide side curves.

Traditional Cross

The simple lines of this frame make it easy to play with different design elements such as color, texture, and large focal beads or stones.

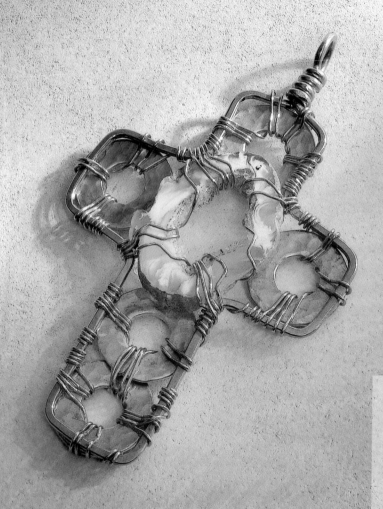

MATERIALS
Wire:
- **10"** 16-gauge round (frame)
- **5–10'** 24- or 26-gauge round (sewing)

Embellishment:
- 18x25mm geode slice
- 5 ¼"-diameter textured copper washers

Finished length: 3"

Frame

Flush-cut 10" of 16-gauge round wire. Smooth the ends.

For this design, you may find it helpful to first make a paper template of the measurements on paper and then transfer the marks to the wire with a permanent marker **[a]**. Mark a center point. One one side, mark at these points from the center point: ¼", 1", ½", ½", ½", ½", and ¼". Repeat to mark the side opposite the center point at the same intervals so you have matching pairs of marks.

Use flatnose pliers to make all the bends as you shape the cross. Every bend will be at a 90-degree angle. First, make a 90-degree bend at the first pair of marks. This is the bottom of the cross **[b]**.

At the next pair of marks (1" away), bend the ends 90 degrees as shown **[c]**.

At the next pair of marks (½" away), bend the ends 90 degrees as shown **[d]**. At the next pair of marks (½" away), bend the ends

90 degrees as shown **[e]**. The ends will cross each other.

At the next pair of marks (½" away), bend the ends 90 degrees as shown. The ends will point up **[f]**.

At the next pair of marks (½" away), bend the ends 90 degrees as shown **[g]**. The ends will cross each other.

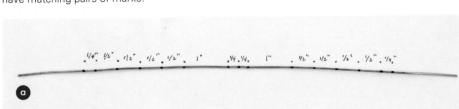

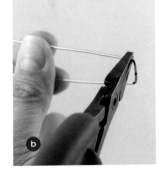

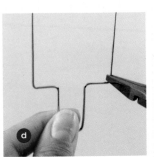

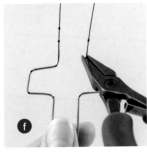

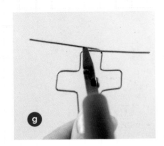

At the next pair of marks (1/2" away), bend one end 90 degrees as shown **[h]**.

With chainnose pliers, wrap the end that extends to the side at least two times around the end pointing up **[i]**. Trim the excess wrapping and smooth any burs.

Using the chasing hammer and the bench block, work-harden and flatten the entire frame except the wrapped neck.

Bail
Make a wrapped-loop bail **[j]**.

Embellishment
To embellish the cross frame, I used a geode slice with a large opening in the center and copper washers that I textured with a hammer.

Using short (4–10") lengths of 24- or 26-gauge wire, sew the washers to the frame, textured side up and layered behind the frame **[k]**. Make at least three to five wraps to anchor each washer.

Sew the geode slice to the center front of the pendant, layered over the frame. Layering the embellishments adds dimension and accentuates the geode slice **[l]**. Make small bends in the sewing wire to tighten the geode slice to the frame and add texture **[m]**.

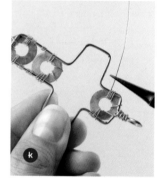

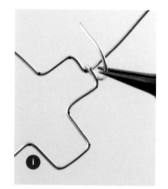

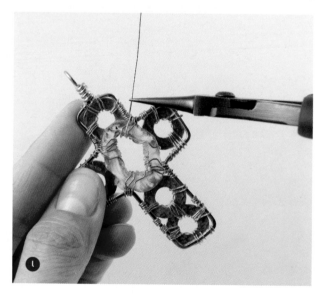

design
options

For a sleek, all-metal look, shape 16-gauge round wire into curves that follow the cross frame. Flatten the wire shape on the bench block and sew it to the frame.

▼ Emphasize the simple, graceful lines of this design by using the large wire accent technique.

◀ Using all turquoise beads gives this cross an organic, Native American look.

Simply Red-hot Heart

This framed pendant is a versatile Valentine-inspired heart.
The heart shape is a timeless motif that is a favorite of many people.

MATERIALS
- 8x12mm 16-gauge open oval jump ring (bail)

Wire:
- **8"** 16-gauge round (frame)
- **5–10'** 24- or 26-gauge (sewing)
- **10"** 20-gauge round (support)

Bead assortment such as:
- 14mm lampwork disk bead
- 4x10mm tube bead
- 8mm round crystal
- **9** 8mm seed-shaped beads
- **4** 3mm round crystals
- **6** 3mm round beads
- **8** 2mm round copper beads
- **4** 2mm disk beads

Finished length: 2¼" (with dangle)

Frame

Flush-cut 8" of 16-gauge round wire. Smooth the ends.

With permanent marker, mark the center of the wire. Using flatnose pliers, make a 90-degree bend **[a]**.

On one end, make a simple loop and then form an open spiral. Spiral at least twice around **[b]**.

Using your fingers, shape the opposite end into a curve that matches the size of the open spiral **[c]**.

Use flatnose pliers to make a bend as shown at the point that is even with the base of the spiral **[d]**.

With flatnose pliers, make a small spiral at the end of the wire **[e]**.

Using the chasing hammer and the bench block, work-harden and flatten the entire frame. Reshape the frame with your fingers.

Bail

Attach the open oval jump ring to the top small spiral **[f]**.

Embellishment

Choose your bead assortment and audition the beads in the frame. I used a variety of red coral beads, red crystals, a red lampwork disk bead, and copper beads.

Using 20-gauge wire, sew in support wires across the bottom of the heart **[g]**. The support wires strengthen the frame and provide a base for attaching beads.

TIP

Space can add interest to a pendant. Leave some empty spots; you do not have to fill every open space.

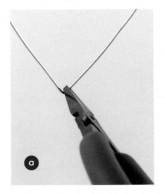
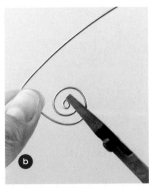
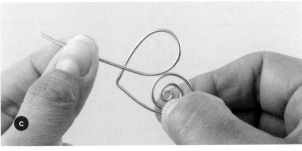

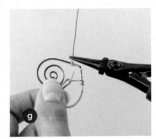

Using short (4–10") lengths of 24- or 26-gauge wire, sew in the beads, beginning with the seed-shaped beads in the spiral [h]. Make at least three to five wraps for each bead. Then sew in the remaining beads [i]. For emphasis, add bends to the wire used to sew in the lampwork disk bead. Add a bead dangle at the bottom [j].

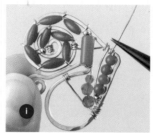

design
options

◀ Echo the heart frame spiral by adding a hammered spiral made from 16-gauge round wire. Finish the look with a spiral dangle.

Create a whimsical black heart using open space and the wire edging technique.

Consider flipping the ▶ frame and using a variety of natural coral beads for a more traditionally rendered organic heart.

Double Triangle Twisted Frame

This framed pendant is one of my favorites. It can be simple and understated or made into a fabulous statement piece, depending on the materials you choose.

MATERIALS

Wire:
- **9"** 16-gauge round (frame)
- **3"** 12-gauge half-round (bail)
- **5–10'** 24- or 26-gauge round (sewing)
- **10"** 18-gauge round (accent)

Bead assortment such as:
- **2** 15mm disk beads
- **2** 8mm round beads
- 8mm oval freshwater pearl
- **2** 4mm round beads
- **6** 4mm bicone crystals
- **2** 6mm bicone crystals

Finished length: 2¾"

Frame

Flush-cut 9" of 16-gauge round wire. Smooth the ends. With permanent marker, mark 2" from one end. Make an open spiral, spiraling to the mark **[a]**. This is the top of the pendant.

Mark ½" from the first mark. Using flatnose pliers, make a 90-degree bend at this point as shown **[b]**. Mark 1¼" from the bend. Using roundnose pliers, make a soft V-shape bend up toward the spiral **[c]**. Mark 1¼" from the V and make another soft bend as shown **[d]**.

Mark 1¼" from the last bend. Using flatnose pliers, make a 90-degree bend as shown **[e]**. Make another open spiral from the end of the wire **[f]**. End the spiral at the center bottom of the pendant.

Using the chasing hammer and the bench block, work-harden and flatten the entire frame.

Bail

Use 12-gauge wire to make a half-round bail **[g]**.

Embellishment

Choose your bead assortment and audition the beads in the frame. I used large disk beads, crystals in two sizes, and a pearl as an accent.

Using short (4–10") lengths of the 24 or 26-gauge wire, sew in the beads, starting with the large disk beads. Sew in a disk at each of the widest parts of the V shapes **[h]**. Make three to five wraps for each sewn-in bead. Sew in the remainder of the beads **[i]**. Place the pearl in the center of the frame as the focal bead.

Sew in an 18-gauge accent wire, encircling the pearl and

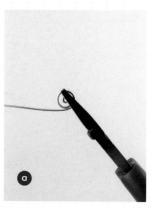

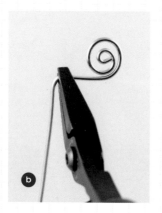

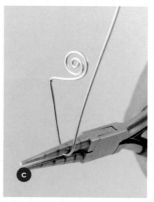

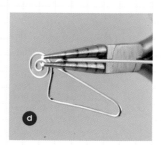

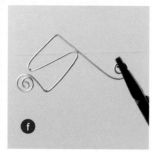

looping over each disk bead. This will emphasize the pearl and add support to the disk beads. To support the frame, sew each spiral to the nearest bend in the frame **[j]**.

design options

An oblong piece of rose quartz and a small oblong drusy sit side by side in this frame. Using maroon crystals and the large wire accent technique, I created three distinct sections of color.

▲ For this delicate pendant, I used less wire and small-scale embellishments, such as the tiny drusy at the pendant bottom.

◀ I found this rough natural drusy on one of my biking rock hunts. I paired it with natural frosted quartz.

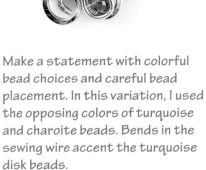

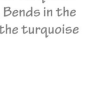

Make a statement with colorful bead choices and careful bead placement. In this variation, I used the opposing colors of turquoise and charoite beads. Bends in the sewing wire accent the turquoise disk beads.

Shining Star

The stars in the night sky inspired this pendant project. With this frame, you too can add a little sparkle to your wardrobe.

MATERIALS

Wire:
- **10"** 16-gauge round (frame)
- **3"** 12-gauge half-round (bail)
- **5–10'** 24- or 26-gauge round (sewing)

Bead assortment such as:
- 15mm glass lampwork disk bead
- **5** 6mm round crystals
- **5** 2mm round pearls
- **10** 2mm copper beads

Finished length: 2½"

Frame

Flush-cut 10" of 16-gauge round wire. Smooth the ends.

With permanent marker, mark 1" from the end of the wire. Then mark every 1½" from the first mark until you have made a total of six marks. (You may find it helpful to make a paper template first and transfer the marks to the wire.)

Using flatnose pliers, starting at the first 1½" mark, make a 45-degree bend **[a]**. Make three more bends as shown, all curving inward **[b, c, d]**. The wires will cross and will loosely resemble a star.

With flatnose pliers, bend the ends so they are perpendicular to each other **[e]**.

With chainnose pliers, wrap the end that extends to the side at least twice around the end that points up. Trim the excess wrapping wire and smooth any burs **[f]**.

Make an open spiral at the top of the pendant **[g]**.

Using the chasing hammer and the bench block, work-harden and flatten the entire frame except for the wrapped neck and the points where the wire overlaps itself.

Bail

Use the 12-gauge wire to make a half-round bail and attach it to the top of the spiral.

Embellishment

Choose your bead assortment and audition the beads in the frame. I used a lampwork disk bead, small pearls, crystals, and small copper beads.

Using your fingers, shape the points of the star into equal sizes. Using the 24- or 26-gauge round wire, sew together the five points where the wire overlaps itself. This will add strength to and hold the star shape as you work on the pendant.

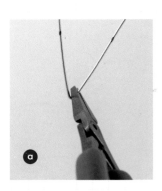

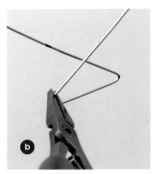

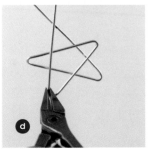

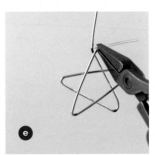

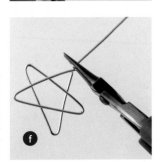

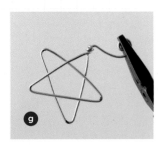

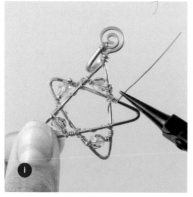

Using short (4–10") lengths of 24- or 26-gauge wire, sew in the beads, starting with the crystals within the point segments **[h, i]**. Make three to five wraps for each bead. Sew in pearls at the tips of each point. In the center of the star, sew in the lampwork disk bead, adding small bends in the wire over the bead **[j]**.

design
options

I wrapped 24-gauge round wire around each point and made a small star in the center of the pendant.

▲ Pearls, crystals, and edging add bling and sparkle to this star.

▲ The bold pearls and cane glass bead add structure and give this star pizzazz.

◀ Metal zigzags, a metal spiral, and a red crystal bead at its center give this star a contemporary look.

Butterfly Dazzle

This project shows you how to construct a basic butterfly frame.
You can adapt the shape and embellish with beads to match the colors of your
favorite butterfly. Small frames can become dangles for a bracelet or earrings.

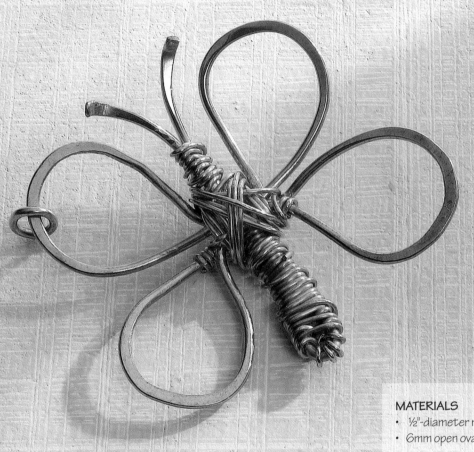

MATERIALS
- ½"-diameter round dowel
- 6mm open oval jump ring

Wire:
- **14"** 16-gauge round (frame)
- **5'** 22-gauge round (wrapping)

Finished length: 1¾"

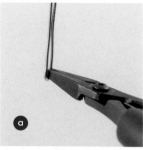

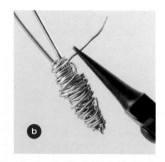

Frame

Flush-cut 14" of 16-gauge round wire. Smooth the ends.

With permanent marker, mark the center of the wire and fold the wire in half **[a]**. This is the bottom of the butterfly's abdomen.

Mark the wire ¾" from the bottom fold. Cut the 22-gauge round wire into two

30" pieces. Using chainnose pliers, wrap one of the pieces around the bent wire, starting from the bottom and working up to the mark. For a thin abdomen, don't use all the wire; for a thicker abdomen, wrap all of the wire **[b]**.

With chainnose pliers, make a bend on each side of the abdomen **[c]**.

Form each end around the dowel as shown **[d, e]**. These are the lower wings.

With flatnose pliers, bend the ends 90 degrees to align with the abdomen **[f]**. Form each end around the dowel as shown **[g]**. These are the top wings.

With flatnose pliers, again bend the wires 90 degrees to align with the abdomen **[h]**. These are the antennae.

Shape the wings with your fingers and finish wrapping the rest of the body with the remaining 22-gauge round wire **[i]**.

Trim the antennae to the length you like. With chainnose pliers, slightly bend the tips of each one.

Using the chasing hammer and the bench block, work-harden and flatten the wings and antennae.

Bail

Attach a 6mm open oval jump ring to the top of a wing as the bail **[j]**.

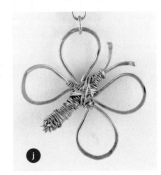

design
options

▲ I added beaded edging and made the wings larger and rounder to encircle lovely large crystal shapes.

▲ Solid-color disk beads add color to these wings.

◀ Use more wire and elongate the abdomen and wings to transform the butterfly into a dragonfly. Sew in small black onyx and crystal beads to accent the abdomen and wings.

Eliminate the abdomen and use bold colors for a stylized butterfly. Attach chain directly to the antennae.

Contemporary Cross

Abstract lines and unusual pearl shapes are graceful and elegant in this cross frame.

MATERIALS

Wire:
- **14"** 16-gauge round (frame)
- **5'** 24- or 26-gauge round (sewing)
- **3"** 12-gauge half-round (bail)

Bead assortment such as:
- **4** 12mm teardrop coin pearls
- **8mm** pearl
- **2** 6mm pearls
- **2** 4mm pearls
- **4** 3mm pearls
- **5** 2mm pearls

Finished length: 3½"

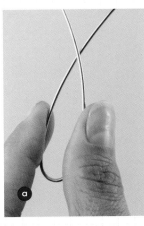

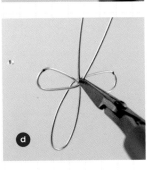

Frame

Flush-cut 14" of 16-gauge round wire. Smooth the ends.

With permanent marker, mark the center of the wire. Make another mark 1½" away on each side of the center mark.

Using the large jaw of the bail-making pliers, make a loop on the center mark. This is the bottom of the cross **[a]**.

At the 1½" marks, use flatnose pliers to bend the ends 90 degrees toward each other **[b]**.

From each bend, mark 1". On the marks, use the large jaw of the bail-making pliers to form the side loops **[c]**.

On each side, use flatnose pliers to bend the ends up as shown **[d]**.

Mark 1" from the last bends. Use the bail-making pliers to shape the top loops at the marks **[e]**. The ends will cross each other as shown;

this is the center of the top loop.

Where the ends cross, make a 90-degree bend in one wire and bend the other wire to the side so the ends are perpendicular **[f]**.

With chainnose pliers, wrap the wire that extends out at least twice around the end pointing up. Trim the excess wrapping wire and smooth any burs. Use the remaining end to make an eye loop **[g]**.

Bail

Use the 12-gauge wire to make a half-round bail and attach it to the eye loop.

Using the chasing hammer and the bench block, work-harden and flatten the curved parts of the frame, avoiding the points where the wire overlaps.

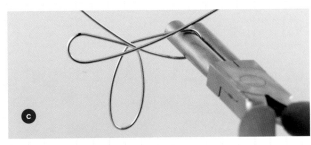

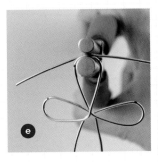

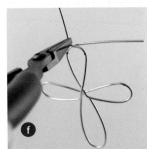

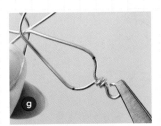

Use 24-gauge round wire to wrap the center of the cross as shown **[h]**.

Embellishment

Choose your bead assortment and audition the beads in the frame. I used a variety of sizes and shapes of pearls.

Using short (4–10") lengths of 24- or 26-gauge wire, begin sewing in the pearls. Sew in the coin pearls and each large round pearl first in each looped section. Then sew in the smaller side pearls **[i, j]**. Make three to five wraps for each sewn-in bead **[k]**.

design
options

The spiny blue oyster shell beads in this variation remind me of the cool hues of the sea.

◀ This bright cross is made with rows of sewn-in small ruby beads. I squared the cross ends with flatnose pliers.

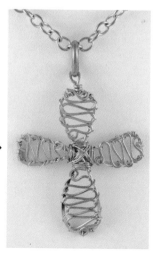

Curve, taper, and flatten ▶ 16-gauge round wire shapes for each arm and sew them to the frame. This technique works well for smaller crosses.

Build Your Own
Drilled-bead Projects

There is a lot more you can do with a large drilled stone or bead than simply stringing it! The three projects in this section offer ideas for creating focal pendants with beads that are drilled in different ways.

This dragon skin turquoise pendant incorporates a stone that's drilled top to bottom and one that's drilled front to back. On top I used the double wrapped loop technique. For the lower stone, I used a wrapped loop bail finished with a spiral, and I attached a spiral to the inside of the wire that passes through the hole. The first two projects in this section teach the techniques used in this pendant.

Big-bead Pendant

Transform a large focal bead into a gorgeous pendant with wire and bead dangle embellishments. These dramatic pendants can be quite elaborate with spirals, twists, and complementary beads.

MATERIALS

Wire:
- **10"** 16- or 18-gauge round (frame)
- **3"** 12-gauge half-round (bail)

Other materials:
- 19x12mm large-hole gemstone bead
- 2 4mm round crystals
- 2 headpins

Finished length: 1¾"

Frame

Flush-cut 10" of wire and smooth the ends. (Choose the wire gauge that fits through the hole in the bead.) This will give you enough wire to add embellishments.

TIP
The look of heavy-gauge wire is well suited to a substantial stone bead with a large hole that can accommodate the thick wire.

Determine how the bead will be oriented in the pendant: top, bottom, front, and back. Each stone has character, and your choice can show off its beauty.

Use permanent marker to mark 3½" from one end. This end will form the top of the pendant. Place the wire through the stone with the mark just above the top hole in the bead **[a]**.

Use your fingers to make a sharp bend just below the bead so the wire runs up the back of the bead and both ends are pointing up **[b]**. Bend this wire tightly over the top of the bead **[c]**.

With chainnose pliers, wrap the bent wire end tightly

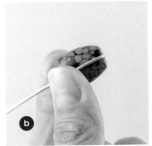

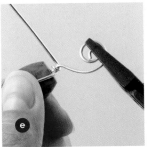

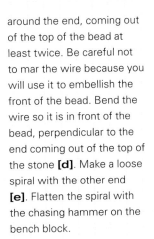

around the end, coming out of the top of the bead at least twice. Be careful not to mar the wire because you will use it to embellish the front of the bead. Bend the wire so it is in front of the bead, perpendicular to the end coming out of the top of the stone **[d]**. Make a loose spiral with the other end **[e]**. Flatten the spiral with the chasing hammer on the bench block.

Bail
Use the 12-gauge wire to make a half-round bail. Attach it to the top of the spiral **[f]**.

Embellishment
Make a large, loose loop as shown **[g]**.

Make a second loop as shown **[h]**. Make a third loop and add crystal dangles to the second and third loops **[i]**. Flush-cut any excess wire and smooth the ends.

If the wire at the back of the pendant is loose, tighten it by making a small bend at the midpoint.

Press the loops onto the front of the bead. If the loops do not seem to lie flat, you can use chainnose pliers to bend the top of the first loop slightly to make the loops hug the bead.

design
options

For this alternative, make a wrapped-loop bail. Bring the bail wire to the front and use it along with the back wire to make spirals and add accent bead dangles.

▲ Make a wrapped loop at the bottom of the pendant, and then make loops bringing the bottom wire back to the top. Attach a crystal dangle to the bottom loop.

For a very dainty drop, ▶ use a smaller bead and make a simple spiral at the top.

▲ Consider sewing complementary crystals to two of the loops. Use a third crystal for a dangle.

Front-drilled Pendant

Many large, somewhat flat gemstone beads have a hole
that's drilled front to back. In this project, you'll learn how to transform these
gorgeous beads into pendants!

MATERIALS
Wire:
- **14"** 16-gauge round (bail and
  spiral dangle)

Other materials:
- 32x18mm large-hole front-
  drilled gemstone bead
- painters tape

Finished length: 2¼"

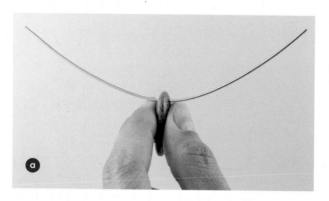

Frame

Flush-cut 8" of 16-gauge round wire. Smooth the ends. Mark 4" from one end. Choose which side will be the front of the pendant, and place a small piece of painters tape on the front bottom of the pendant. Place the wire through the hole in the pendant with the mark at the center of the hole **[a]**.

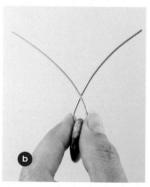

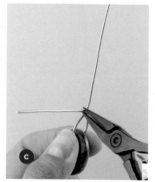

Push the ends together so they cross **[b]**. With flatnose pliers, bend the ends so they are perpendicular **[c]**.

With chainnose pliers, wrap the end that extends to the side at least twice around the other end. Be careful not to mar the wire. Bring the wire to the front of the bead (the side marked with painters tape) and make a small spiral **[d]**. Press the spiral against the wire coming out of the front of the pendant.

Bail

Make an eye loop bail **[e, f]**.

Embellishment

Using 6" of 16-gauge round wire, make a spiral with a simple loop at the top. Attach the spiral to the front of the pendant, opening and closing the loop portion of the spiral as you would a jump ring **[g]**.

design options

◀ Reuse reclaimed jewelry in your designs! I used a copper cross from a piece of jewelry I purchased at a garage sale.

Accent a drilled bead with a sterling silver spiral.

◀ This long piece of picture jasper is enhanced with a simple crystal dangle.

▲ Dark brown agate is accentuated with sterling silver. I dangled a modified version of the Basic Twisted Frame from the top.

Side-drilled Pendant

Gemstones that are drilled side to side can be challenging to work with. Here is one pretty solution.

MATERIALS

Wire:
- **7"** 16- or 18-gauge round (use the gauge that fits through the bead hole)
- **36"** 26-gauge round (edging)

Other materials:
- 25x18mm large-hole side-drilled stone
- **12** 3mm freshwater pearls
- painters tape

Finished length: 1⅞"

Frame

Flush-cut 7" of 16-gauge round wire. Smooth the ends.

Choose which side will be the front of your pendant, and place a small piece of painters tape on the front bottom of the bead. Center the wire in the hole of the bead **[a]**.

With your fingers, push the ends together so they cross **[b]**. With flatnose pliers, bend the wire ends so they are perpendicular **[c]**.

With chainnose pliers, wrap the end that extends to the side at least twice around the other end. Be careful not to mar the wire because you will use it to make a small spiral. Bring the wrapping wire to the front and make a small open spiral **[d]**.

Bail

Make an eye loop bail **[e, f]**.

Embellishment

Using 26-gauge round wire, edge the front open spiral with freshwater pearls. Sew a freshwater pearl into the center of the spiral **[g]**.

design options

Take the idea further by using the bail wrap wire to make a large loop in front and a smaller loop draped to one side. I used pearls and a sea agate bead to enhance this green drusy. ▶

▼ An elongated bail with zigzagging curves paired with a complementary copper dangle tops this variscite pendant.

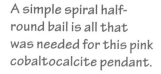

A simple spiral half-round bail is all that was needed for this pink cobaltocalcite pendant.

A simple loop that ▶ mimics the shape of this cobaltocalcite bead makes the design flow. Consider sewing a bead into the loop.

I used a double spiral to ▶ add size and dimension to this chrysocolla pendant.

▲ Sterling silver brings out the beautiful blue of this chrysocolla bead.

Build Your Own
Wire Bezel Projects

Learn how to turn any cabochon into a pendant by framing it with a simple wire bezel. In this section, you'll also get bonus ideas for embellishing bails.

I wanted to make this vivid dichroic cabochon a bit more formal, so I accented the bezel with black crystals encircled by silver wire. I placed one crystal low to draw the eye to the cab.

Basic Wire Bezel

After you have mastered the techniques presented in this project,
you'll be able to make a simple, beautiful pendant starting with almost any shape
of cabochon. To keep things simple at first, use a symmetrical oval cabochon.
Asymmetrical or faceted stones are a little more challenging to frame.

MATERIALS

Wire:
- **42"** 20-gauge square (bezel)
- **20"** 20-gauge half-round (wrapping)
- **5"** 22-gauge square (bail wrap)

Other materials:
- 30x20mm oval cabochon
- painters tape

Finished length: 2"

Bezel

1 To determine how much wire to cut for the bezel and bail, measure the circumference of the cabochon by noting the starting point and rolling the cab along a ruler until you return to the original point. A 30x20mm stone has a circumference of about 3".

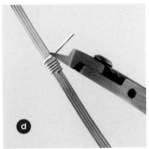

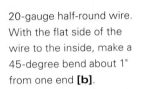

2 Add 7" and cut three pieces of 20-gauge square wire to that length. Add 3" and cut another piece to that length. (You'll use the extra 3" to make a secure wrap at the top of your cab.)

TIP

You may need more or fewer pieces of wire, depending on the thickness of the cabochon. Check how many stacked wires it takes to cover the edge of the stone, and add one more piece.

3 Align the wires flat and flush, placing the longest piece in the middle. Bundle the wires and place a piece of painters tape around them. Wrap tape on three or four more spots on the bundle, placing the tape flags in the same direction **[a]**.

4 Measure and mark the center of the bundle with permanent marker. Cut 4" of 20-gauge half-round wire. With the flat side of the wire to the inside, make a 45-degree bend about 1" from one end **[b]**.

5 Place this hook slightly to the left of the center mark on the bundle and hold it in place with your thumb. Begin wrapping the long end snugly around the bundle. Make the wraps close together. After every two to three wraps, use flatnose pliers to press the wire flat (crimp it) to the bundle. Be careful not to twist or bend the wire as you wrap it around the bundle. Make at least five wraps **[c]**.

6 Use flush cutters to trim the ends of the wrapping wire. Make both cuts on the same side of the bundle. This will become the inside of your bezel wrap; the cab will press against these cuts and hold them in place **[d, e]**.

7 Tear off a piece of painters tape the same length as the wire bundle. Fold it in half lengthwise, sticky side together. This marker will help you decide where to place the other bindings.

8 Gently press the tape around the cab to determine the placement of two additional bindings. Mark the spots on the tape **[f]**.

TIP

Bindings don't have to be symmetrical; I often accentuate a feature of a cab with asymmetrical placement.

9 Transfer the marks to the bundle **[g]**. Cut two 4" pieces of 20-gauge half-round wire. Wrap the two new marks as before, keeping all the end cuts on the same side of the bundle.

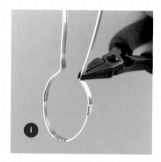
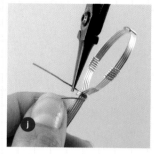
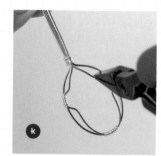

10 With the tape flags facing up, shape and press the bundle up and around the cab and mark where the ends cross. Make sure the end cuts all face to the inside, against the cab **[h]**. Putting a gentle curve in the bundle before pressing it to the shape of the cab will make this easier.

11 With flatnose pliers, bend the ends up at the marks **[i]**. Tape the bent ends together to hold them in place.

12 Use 22-gauge square wire to wrap the top where the ends are bent up. Wrap a minimum of four times around. The last wrap should be at the base of the bail **[j]**.

13 Remove all but one of the tape flags. This flag will remind you which side is the front of the bezel (the side without a flag is the back of the frame). Create the back support bends for your cab: Hold the frame in your hand, place the tip of the flatnose pliers beside one wrapped binding on the back, and grasp only one outside wire and bend it to the inside. Be careful not to change the shape of the bezel as you hold it **[k]**. Repeat this step until you have made at least four bends on the back of the frame. These bends will act as prongs to help hold the cab in the bezel.

14 Place the cab back in the frame. It should fit snugly. Make bends in front of the cab to hold it in place. For this cab, I made gentle curves with two and three of the wires by gently pulling them forward with my fingernails and the flatnose pliers **[l]**.

15 Separate the top wires a little. With four wires in the bundle, this should yield eight top wires. Take the longest of the eight wires and bend it at a 90-degree angle to the top of the cab **[m]**.

TIP
Place a piece of painters tape on this long wire as a reminder not to cut it. It is the top base wrap wire.

Bail
16 Separate the two middle wires from the rest of the wires. (You can mark these with tape to distinguish them from the rest of the top wires. These two wires will later become the bail.) Trim the remaining five wires so they are about ⅛" long. Bend these wires to the side of the bail base and over the bail base wire wrap **[n]**.

17 Wrap the two middle wires together over the small jaw of the bail-making pliers and down to the back of the cab **[o]**.

TIP

Use the larger jaw (or a different size of bail-making pliers) to make other sizes of bails.

18 Hold the two top bail wires against the back of the cab. Wrap the end that is at a 90-degree angle tightly around the wires, starting at the top and wrapping down **[p]**. If you run out of wire, continue wrapping by pulling one of the wires from the back and continuing to wrap. Stop wrapping when the wire reaches the top of the cab and the bottom of the bail. Tuck in the wire at the bottom of the wrap **[q]**.

Embellishment

19 Trim and spiral the wires remaining at the back of the cab **[r]**. With your fingers, separate the bail wires **[s]**.

design options

Pull one of the frame wires free, make a large open spiral, and sew it in place.

▲ I used the bent wire edging to accentuate the green spot in this dichroic glass pendant.

▲ The sterling silver frame and sharply bent wire edging show off this clear blue turquoise cabochon.

▲ Sometimes your beautiful stone has an irregular shape. Make a frame wire into a large spiral accent to balance the shape.

Upside-down Wire Bezel

Express your creativity with an upside-down wire bezel pendant.
Mix this technique with many others for entirely different looks.

MATERIALS
Wire:
- 3½' 20-gauge square (bezel)
- 1½' 20-gauge half-round (wrapping)
- 6" 22-gauge square (bottom wrap)
- 3" 12-gauge half-round (bail)

Other materials:
- 30x20mm oval cabochon
- 4 3mm round crystals (optional)
- painters tape

Finished length: 2¼"

Bezel

1 Measure the circumference of the cabochon by noting the starting point and rolling the cab along a ruler until you return to the original point. A 30x20mm cab has a circumference of about 3".

2 Add 7" and cut three pieces of 22-gauge square wire to that length. Add 2" and cut another piece to that length. (You'll use the extra 2" to make a center loop for attaching the bail.)

> **TIP**
> **You may need more or fewer pieces of wire, depending on the thickness of the cabochon. Check how many stacked wires it takes to cover the edge of the stone, and add one more piece.**

3 Mark the center of the longest piece of wire. Using roundnose pliers, make a loop on the center mark **[a]**. This loop will become the top center of the pendant.

4 Align the wires flat and flush with the looped piece of wire in the middle of the bundle and use a piece of tape to hold them in place. Wrap tape at three or four more spots on the bundle, placing the tape flags in the same direction **[b]**. This will secure the bundle as you work on it.

5 The looped wire should be in the center of your bundle. If necessary, center it by adjusting the bundle wires and tape flags. Cut 6" of 20-gauge half-round wire. With the flat side to the inside, bend the wire into a hook about 1" from one end.

6 Hook the wire on the bundle, slightly to the left of the loop, and hold it in place with your thumb. Begin wrapping the long end of the wire snugly around the bundle. Make sure the wraps are close together. After every few wraps, use flatnose pliers to press the wire flat (crimp it) to the bundle. Be careful not to twist or bend the wire as you wrap it around the bundle. Make at least four wraps **[c]**.

7 Cross the wire through the center loop and wrap it once around the bundle on the opposite side of the loop **[d]**. Use flatnose pliers to crimp the wrapped wire flat.

8 Wrap the wire four more times **[e]**. Trim both ends with flush cutters, placing the cuts on the side of the wire bundle opposite the loop. This will become the inside of the bezel; the cab will press against the ends and hold them in place.

9 Follow steps 8–14 of the Basic Wire Bezel (p. 74). Center the loop at the top of the cab when you mark where the wires cross, and make sure all of the wrapped cuts are on the inside against the cab.

> **TIP**
> **Curve the bundle before pressing it to the shape of the cabochon to make it easier to fit the stone.**

Bail

10 Attach a half-round bail to the loop at the top of the pendant.

11 Turn the pendant upside down so that all the bottom wires are at the top. Separate the wires a little. The four wires of the bundle will yield eight working wires. Bend the longest of the middle wires at a sharp 90-degree angle to the cab as in the Basic Wire Bezel. This will become the wrapping wire.

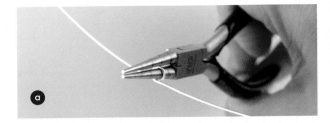

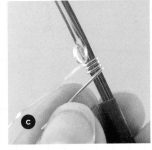

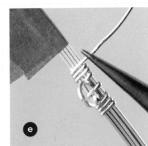

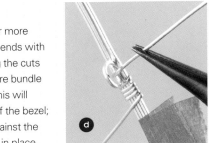

12 Separate the front wire on each side from the rest of the wires. (You can mark these with tape to distinguish them from the rest of the wires.) These will become the loops at the bottom. Trim the remaining wires to about ⅛". Bend these cut wires to the side and over the first half-round wire wrap as in the Basic Wire Bezel.

13 Wrap the wire that is at a 90-degree angle to the side tightly around the trimmed and bent wires as in the Basic Wire Bezel. Stop wrapping when you reach the bottom of the cab. Tuck in the wire at the bottom of the wraps.

Embellishment

14 Using your fingers or roundnose pliers, make two decorative loops in each of the two remaining ends **[f, g]**. Wrap the ends onto the side bezel wires. You may have to gently lift the side bezel wires a little to slide them under each side **[h, i]**.

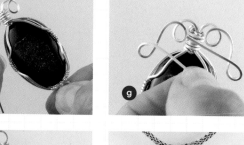

design options

◀ Add crystals to whimsical loops and zigzags to bring out a color in your pendant.

Turning the Upside-down Wire Bezel upside down! Use the loop to attach the dangle or make several loops to add several dangles. Finish the frame top as in the Basic Wire Bezel. ▶

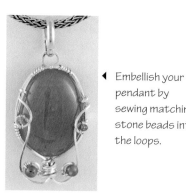

◀ Embellish your pendant by sewing matching stone beads into the loops.

◀ Sew sparkling crystals into your loops.

Close, tight loops create a new look.

Double-ended Wire Bezel

This bezel style is great for accentuating large, bold cabochons.
Two pairs of wire ends offer many possibilities for adding graceful spirals
or other embellishment.

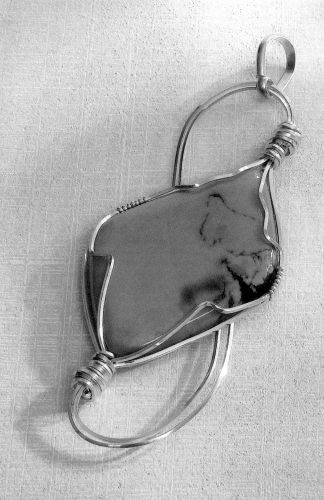

MATERIALS

Wire:
- **8'** 22-gauge square (bezel)
- **24"** 20-gauge half-round
  (wrapping)
- **3"** 12-gauge half-round (bail)

Other materials:
- 45x30mm cabochon
- painters tape

Finished length: 3¼"

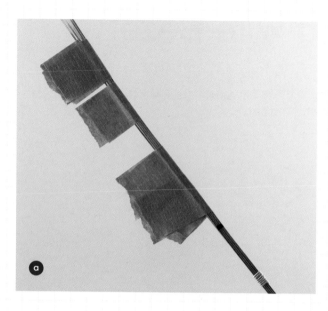

Bezel

This technique is similar to the Basic Wire Bezel except you will have two pairs of ends to work with instead of just one—a set at the top and a set at the bottom of the cab.

1 Measure each side of the cab. Add 8" to the largest of the two measurements and cut eight pieces of 22-gauge square wire to this length.

(For a 45x30mm cab, you will cut eight 12" pieces.)

2 Make two bundles of four pieces of wire each. You will use one bundle for each side of the cab. Follow steps 2–6 of the Basic Wire Bezel (p. 74).

3 Place the wire bundles against each other. Align the center wraps and make sure the trimmed half-round wire

bindings are on the inside and the tape flags are facing the same direction. Tape the two bundles together with the tape at the top of the frame **[a]**.

4 On the now-double bundle, make a mark 5" from the top and tape the two bundles together 1" above this mark. At the 5" mark, wrap the two bundles together using 4" of the half-round wire. Gently spread apart the two bundles and loosely shape the bezel for the cab **[b]**.

5 Position the bezel around the cab. Push the cab into the corner where the two bundles are wrapped together **[c]**.

6 Continue to shape the bezel around the cab and mark the point where the two bundles cross at the bottom of the cab (see step 10 of the Basic Wire Bezel) **[d]**.

7 Bend the wire at the marks and wrap the two bundles together using 4" of the half-round wire as you did at the other end (see step 11 of the Basic Wire Bezel) **[e]**.

8 Follow step 13 and 14 of the Basic Wire Bezel **[f]**.

Note: You will be using three wires at the top and three at the bottom of your pendant for the final wraps.

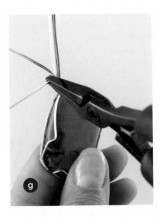

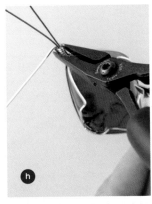

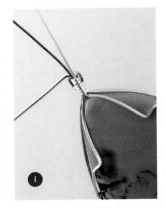

You will bend one of each set of three wires 90 degrees to the side and wrap it around each base at each end at the top and bottom. The other two wires in each set will form side curves for the top and bottom of the cab.

9 At the top of the pendant, bend one of the middle wires 90 degrees to the side and put a piece of tape on it **[g]**.

10 Separate the two front wires and tape them together to separate them from the rest of the wires. Trim the remaining top wires to approximately ⅛" and tuck them down over the base wrap **[h, i]**.

11 Remove the tape from the three remaining wires. Wrap the wire with the 90-degree bend around the bail base at the top of the cabochon **[j]**.

12 Repeat steps 9–11 above for the bottom group of wires. This will leave two wires at the top and two wires at the bottom for the final wraps **[k]**.

13 Curve the top two wires together around to the back of the cabochon **[l]**.

14 Tuck the two wires under the first bend in the back bezel frame and wrap them around the bend in the opposite bezel frame.

Note: You may have to gently lift the back frame bends a bit to attach the two wires **[m]**.

15 Repeat steps 13 and 14 for the bottom two wires.

Bail
16 Attach a half-round bail to the top loops **[n, o]**.

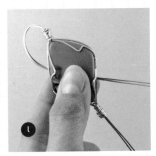

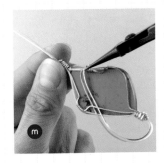

design
options

Balance an oblong stone and build a rich look by using more wires to loop around and across the stone.

This wire bezel lends itself beautifully to three-dimensional pendants because you can wrap wires across the front of the pendant and through or around any dimensional parts of the cabochon.

Simple lines of wire balance the shape and show off the stone's grain lines. ▶

◀ For this large triangular agate drusy, I used a heavier gauge of wire and incorporated freshwater pearls in various rich, chocolatey colors as lovely counterparts to the stone.

Bonus Finishing Techniques for Bezeled Pendants

I love the black, lime-green, and speckles of this glass cabochon. I used techniques described in this section to embellish the top with black onyx beads.

Spiral Away

The spiraling technique allows you to position and shape
the top of your pendant in many different ways.

MATERIALS

Wire:
- **3½'** 20-gauge square (bezel)
- **1½'** 20-gauge half-round (wrapping)
- **5"** 22-gauge square (bail wrap)

Other materials:
- 35x25mm oval cabochon
- painters tape

Finished length: 2½"

Bezel

1 Using a three-wire bundle, follow steps 1–15 of the Basic Wire Bezel (p. 74).

2 Separate the two middle wires from the rest of the wires and wrap painters tape around them.

3 Follow steps 17 and 18 of the Basic Wire Bezel.

Bail

4 This will leave three wires at the top. Spiral one front wire and center it over the base of the wraps at the top **[a, b]**.

5 With one of the remaining top wires, make a large curve around the first spiral. Bring the wire tightly around the back of the cab base and make a small spiral at the front of the cab **[c, d, e]**.

6 With the remaining top wire, make a large curve around the first spiral, opposite the first large curve. Together, the two large curves should resemble a heart **[f]**.

7 Bring the last top wire tightly around the back of the cab base and make another small spiral at the front of the cab **[g]**.

8 Using your fingers or chainnose pliers, position the spirals on the front of the cab **[h, i]**.

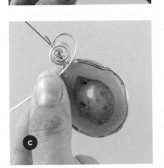

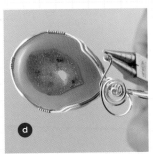

design
options

▲ A simple large curve
on each side of the bail
creates a heart shape
to highlight a fabulous
red cabochon.

▼ A cascade of spirals
continues the illusion of
bubbling liquid within this
glass cab.

Pulling the spirals down
and onto the pendant
accentuates the design.

▲ I balanced the form of this
organically shaped drusy
with off-center loops and
spirals.

▲ A simple spiral crowns this vivid
glass pendant.

Beaded Bail

Use the same accent beads in the rest of your necklace
or in earrings for a coordinated look.

MATERIALS

Wire:
- 46" 20-gauge square (bezel)
- 5" 22-gauge square
  (bail wrap)
- 1½' 20-gauge half-round
  (wrapping)

Other materials:
- 45x25mm rectangular
  cabochon
- 3 6mm round crystals
- painters tape

Finished length: 2½"

Bezel

1 Using a four-wire bundle, follow steps 1–15 of the Basic Wire Bezel (p. 74), adding 3" to the fourth wire (the 90-degree wrapping wire).

Bail

2 Separate the two middle wires from the rest of the wires. Wrap these with painters tape to distinguish them from the rest of the top wires. These wires will become the bail. Trim the wire that is across from the wire bent to 90 degrees to ⅛". Bend it to the side and over the wire wrap as in the Basic Wire Bezel.

3 Follow steps 17 and 18 of the Basic Wire Bezel. You will have four top wires remaining to work as embellishment.

4 String a bead on one of the front wires **[a]**.

5 Hold the bead where you want it to remain and wrap the wire tightly once around the bead. Wrap the remaining wire around the bail base and tuck it in. Trim the wire if needed **[b]**.

6 Repeat step 5 for the remaining two wires and add small loops or spirals. Trim the remaining wire before you tuck it in **[c, d]**.

7 Follow step 19 of the Basic Wire Bezel **[e]**.

design options

▼ Combine encircled crystal beads with spirals for a fabulous look.

This **chocolate-color drusy is elegant topped with tightly wrapped crystals in a matching color.**

▲ Black crystals dress up this green aventurine.

A wild color ▶ combination wants to be the star of this show, so I used matching blue crystals to add sparkle without detracting from the cab.

▲ A variety of crystal colors accentuates the glass cabochon, and large and small loops center the beads.

▲ Green crystals complement this green turquoise cabochon.

Spin Sensations

This project will teach you how to add a sleek, decorative spiral
to finish off a bail.

MATERIALS
Wire:
- **3½'** 20-gauge square (bezel)
- **5"** 22-gauge square
  (bail wrap)
- **1½'** 20-gauge half-round
  (wrapping)

Other materials:
- 45x25mm oval cabochon
- painters tape

Finished length: 2³/₈"

Bezel

1 Using 20-gauge square wire, create a three-wire bundle, adding 3" to one wire. Follow steps 1–15 of the Basic Wire Bezel (p. 74).

2 Separate the two middle wires from the rest of the wires. Wrap tape around them to distinguish them from the rest of the wires. Trim the wire directly across from the wire at a 90-degree angle to ⅛" and tuck it down to the side.

Bail

3 Follow steps 17 and 18 of the Basic Wire Bezel. Two wires will remain **[a]**.

4 Press the front two wires together. Place your thumb on the two wires at the bail base **[b]**.

5 Using your fingers to hold the wire together as one, tightly spiral the wires, keeping your thumb in place as you make the first spiral **[c]**.

6 Make two more spirals with both wires **[d, e]**.

7 Wrap the wires around the base of the bail and tuck them in **[f, g]**.

design options

Carry the look further by adding more spirals.

▼ I kept things simple at the top of this pendant so the eye can easily follow the shape of this dinosaur bone fossil cabochon.

▼ Use two of the top wires to create free-form loops down the sides of the pendant to extend the flowing lines.

▲ This stone was shaped to have more crystal drusy on one side. The technique helped me accent the area with less drusy.

▲ Spiral the wire, drape it to one side, and add a small spiral with a crystal dangle.

▲ Separate one wire from the bundle and make loops that reflect the spirals in the bail. Capture matching crystals along the wire.

▲ Spiral the wire, drape it to one side of the pendant, and sew it to the bezel edging.

Resources

It's always good to begin with your local bead and craft stores when acquiring tools and supplies for wirework. I also encourage you to seek out bead shows in your area—you can learn a lot by visiting booths and talking with artists and vendors.

Here is a list of some of my other favorite suppliers—all but one are online and accessible to you no matter where in the world you are.

Ace Hardware
acehardware.com

Bastet's Beads
bastetsbeads.com

Boerne Rock Shop
boernerockshop.com

Bronwen Heilman
bronwenheilman.com

Eurotool
eurotool.com

Fire Mountain Gems and Beads
firemountaingems.com

Harbor Freight
harborfreight.com

Intrinsic Trading
512-828-0540 (Round Rock, Texas)

Lumina Porcelain
luminainspirations.com

Original's Beads and Gems
originalstexas.com

Otto Frei
ottofrei.com

Rio Grande
riogrande.com

Ron Talhern Designer Cabochons
angelafowler.com

Rupia Peché Polymer Clay
rupia.etsy.com

Weir Studios Glass
weirstudios.com

Acknowledgments

I would like to thank my husband, Blake, for his constant support and encouragement of my work; Jeff Ramirez for his photography skills and help; and my family for their encouragement throughout this project. I would also like to thank my editor, Mary Wohlgemuth, and the fabulous Kalmbach team for their invaluable help and support.

From Kimberly

Designing beaded and wirework jewelry gives me great satisfaction and a creative outlet. For me, it's relaxing and rewarding to work on and complete a project. I love to incorporate a variety of metals, glass, crystals, beads, wire, semiprecious stones, and cabochons to create unique pieces. There is joy in working with exquisite materials and in my ability to create whatever my imagination suggests. My designs are greatly influenced by ancient art and nature. My favorite artist is Alexander Calder because his jewelry and artwork have inspired me to think without limit.

I have been beading and working with wire since my childhood. I attended college art classes and worked in different media such as wire, clay, and paint. After graduating from Baylor University and getting married, my family and my career in education took me away from my artwork. Years passed until I neared the end of my career and I renewed my passion for working with beads, stone, and wire. Since then, my project articles have been published in *Bead&Button* magazine, *Wirework* magazine, and the compilation books *Creative Chain Mail Jewelry* and *Creative Beading*.

When I am not teaching jewelry making or showing and selling my work at jewelry shows, I enjoy rock hunting, reading, and dirt bike riding. I can get to many hard-to-reach places to hunt for rocks much easier on my dirt bike than on foot, and my backpack can hold many specimens—including some that get incorporated in my jewelry.

More dazzling designs for beads and wire!

Explore your creativity and expand your skills by combining beads and wire for beautiful results! Plenty of projects for beginners as well as seasoned wireworkers will help you develop techniques that you can use to create your own artistic wire jewelry!

64186
$21.95

62649
$21.95

HILLSBORO PUBLIC LIBRARIES
Hillsboro, OR
Member of Washington County
www.facebook.com/KalmbachJewelryBooks
COOPERATIVE LIBRARY SERVICES

 www.pinterest.com/kalmbachjewelry

P17675

2XBB